THE LOST KINGDOMS
OF AFRICA
BLACK AFRICA BEFORE 1600

Written by:
Stuart Kallen

Published by Abdo & Daughters, 6535 Cecilia Circle, Edina, Minnesota 55439

Library bound edition distributed by Rockbottom Books, Pentagon Tower, P.O. Box 36036, Minneapolis, Minnesota 55435

Library of Congress Number: 90-083615   ISBN: 1-56239-016-3

Inside Photos by: Bettmann Archive pgs. 4, 7, 19, 26, 35
              Globe Photo's pgs. 9, 16, 21, 22, 24, 29, 37
              Frederic Lewis pgs. 34, 40, 41, 42, 43, 44, 45

Cover Illustrations by: Marlene Kallen

Edited by: Rosemary Wallner

TABLE OF CONTENTS

4

INTRODUCTION

For hundreds of years, Africa and its people have been a mystery to the rest of the world. Early European explorers reported tall, stone cities of wealth and comfort along Africa's East Coast. They went ashore and found people who knew as much about the stars and planets as they did. Vasco da Gama, a Portuguese explorer, reported that the Africans that he met were very civilized. In fact, they snubbed the Europeans for behaving rudely.

In 1518, an explorer told Pope Leo X about the ancient African city of Timbuktu. The city had so many scholars, the explorer said, that the main business activity there was selling books.

Whatever the Europeans thought about Africa began to change with the slave trade in the 1400's. Once the Europeans started kidnapping Africans and selling them as slaves, much of Africa and its people was changed forever. The Europeans also distorted facts about Africa and made up lies to justify their evil actions. Centuries later, the truth about ancient Africa is being discovered by scholars and scientists.

The people of Africa have had a long and exciting history. They have helped mankind become the most successful creature on earth. Early Africans created cultures, civilizations, governments, and systems of thought that were equal to, if not better than, any other civilization. The African people's passionate spirituality helped them create artwork and music unique to mankind.

In this book, we will discover the glorious cities and the amazing civilizations of Africa before the Europeans arrived.

CHAPTER 1
THE ROOTS OF HUMANITY

The Bones of Our Ancestors

About 33 million years ago, a nine-pound animal climbed through the trees in a tropical forest in North Africa. This fruit-eating creature had monkeylike limbs and apelike teeth. Although the animal looked more like a cat, its bone structure was related to humans. The remains of this animal were discovered in 1985. Scientists believe that the animal is the oldest known direct ancestor to man. Scientists call it the "dawn ape."

7

About 1.6 million years ago, a twelve-year-old boy died in the mud and reeds surrounding Kenya's Lake Turkana. Centuries passed as hippopotamus and elephants trampled the boy's bones into the mud. In 1984, the bones were found and pieced together by *anthropologists*. (Scientists who dig up fossils and study ancient human cultures.) The boy is the best preserved and most complete skeleton of early humans ever found.

Because of these and other discoveries, anthropologists believe that every human on Earth has its roots in Africa. The exact birth of mankind is still a mystery. But scientists are sure that manlike creatures were using fire and making tools in Africa millions of years ago.

Through ice ages, floods, fire, and drought, early humans changed as the centuries passed. Around 12,000 years ago, human beings much like modern people lived in Africa. These people had stone tools, knew how to trap and kill animals, and even had pets. From this period the evolution of humans is easier to follow into the modern world. Early humans painted on caves, made pottery and built homes that *archaeologists* (scientists who study ancient people and their cultures) are studying today. After hundreds-of-millions of years of the earth's history, humans had arrived to multiply and populate the earth.

The Climate Changes

Around 8,000 years ago, most Africans lived in the area that is today the Sahara Desert. There, in an area the size of the United States, modern African culture was born. (The entire African continent is three times larger than the United States.) At that time, the climate in this area was wet. The land was green and fertile. Lush, green forests teemed with animals and hundreds of rivers splashed with fish. Many generations of hunters, farmers, and herdsmen roamed the land. These people lived in caves where they painted images on the walls. Hundreds of beautiful cave paintings still exist today.

About 4,000 years ago, the climate of Africa began to change. Humans cut down the forests and their cattle chewed away the ground cover. The land began to dry up. Soon, rain stopped falling and the remaining forests began to die. Slowly, vast grasslands turned to sandy deserts. The fish and animals died, and the people who hunted them were forced to move away.

The people moved in three different directions, taking with them their customs, their memories, and their gods. Some people went to the fertile land along the Nile in southern Egypt. There, they merged with the pyramid building cultures of ancient Egypt. Others moved north and merged with the people around the Mediterranean Sea. Others went south into the heart of the wild African continent.

The Sahara Desert Divides Africa

When the rain stopped falling, around 4,000 years ago, the Sahara Desert began to grow. Blowing and drifting sand covered huge area of Africa. The people north of the Sahara enjoyed uninterrupted contact with other cultures. North African culture merged with the Middle East and the Mediterranean. For people who lived south of the Sahara, however, life was quite different.

The area south of the Sahara Desert (called the sub-Sahara) is twice as big as the United States. The early humans had a difficult time surviving in most of the sub-Sahara. The landscape had variety — mountains, vast grasslands, wide rivers, lush forests — but none of these areas were helpful to humans.

The grasslands fried under a burning sun six months of the year, then flooded with pouring rain the other six months. The mountains were covered with thorns and rocks, all baking in the intense heat.

11

The tropical forests of Africa were dark, wet places full of danger and disease. In some places it rained up to eight feet a year. The dense forest blocked out the sun giving the appearance of unending dusk. Snakes, insects, and wild animals discouraged the bravest soul. The African tsetse fly carried sleeping sickness. The tsetse's bite caused its victims to go to sleep and never wake up. Soon, they died. Mosquitoes swarmed everywhere carrying malaria and yellow fever.

Kingdoms Grow Out of the Jungle

Africans learned how to live in harmony with nature. They learned to combat disease with herbal medicine. They developed methods for raising cattle and growing crops. They learned how to mine metals and make them into tools and jewelry. They mastered hunting in the grasslands and deep jungles. They forged complex religions to worship the natural spirits. And they built cities, states, and kingdoms.

When Africans learned to forge metal about 2,000 years ago, their society changed. Iron made hunting and farming easier. The population increased because more food was available. Soon, central and southern Africa was filled with travelers looking for places to start their own societies.

The country of Africa became thousands of isolated societies living on a huge area of land. Because of this, there were over 1,000 different languages in Africa and as many systems of behavior and belief. Some of those systems produced societies that were as marvelous and beautiful as any in Europe.

By the tenth century, African cities were bustling with merchants, artists, laborers, and scholars. Feasts, celebrations, and family gatherings filled peoples' free time. Busy cities traded with one another over well-traveled roads. Africans supplied Europe with a steady supply of gold.

Over the centuries, people have told many myths and false stories about Africa. Some of what is in this book is information that has been pieced together by archaeologists during the last one hundred years. Stories and songs passed down by word of mouth from one generation to the next also provide a glimpse at the distant past. Ancient cave paintings have been discovered in Africa that show beautiful portraits of men and women, scenes of warfare, and peaceful villages, gods, and godesses. There are also masks, dolls, and clothing used in religious ceremonies. By all accounts, Africa was in its golden age when the European slave traders arrived in the 1400's. A golden age that would soon turn to dust.

CHAPTER 2
THE MERCHANT KINGDOMS OF AFRICA

Ghana

It is said that Kanissa'ia, the King of Ghana, had 1,000 horses. Each horse had a mattress to sleep on and three servants to tend to it. Every evening the king would come out of his palace and talk to his subjects. One thousand logs created a roaring fire. The king sat upon a throne of gleaming gold while food was prepared for 1,000 people.

The kingdom of Ghana was built on the Niger River in present-day Mali. (The present-day country of Ghana is about 800 miles south of the ancient kingdom.) Ghana was the first in a series of commercial empires that were built on the grasslands of north-central Africa in an area known as the Sudan. The kingdoms of Ghana first rose to power around the year 700 and disappeared around 1200. What we know of the history of Ghana is based on the writings of Arab travelers.

The power of iron, gold, and salt fueled the rise of the kingdom of Ghana. Iron allowed the people of Ghana to make swords, daggers, iron weapons, and arrows. An Arab scholar wrote in the year 1067 that, "the king of Ghana could put two hundred thousand warriors in the field, more than forty thousand of them armed with bows and arrows." Another scholar wrote that Ghana's neighbors, "know not iron, and fight with bars of ebony wood. The Ghanians defeat them because they fight with swords and lances." With that kind of fighting power, Ghana quickly overran its neighbors and took control over their resourses, the main one being gold.

Along the Sengal river, southwest of Ghana, lived a tribe of people who loved salt. These people were of the Ferawi (pronounced Fur-ah'-we) tribe. The Ferawi's had no salt but had mines filled with gold. They loved salt so much that they would trade one ounce of their gold for one ounce of salt.

North of Ghana lay vast salt mines. On camelback, Arab traders from the Middle East would journey thousands of miles to Ghana. They wanted to buy gold. The Arab traders would bring salt to Ghana from the north and trade it for Ferawi gold from the south. Thus, Ghana was a crossroads for trade between the people who wanted salt and people who wanted gold. The Ghanians controlled the roads that the Arabs used. The Arabs had to pay taxes to the Ghanians in gold, copper, cloth, and dried friuit.

15

The Ghanians built large, comfortable cities of stone. Their markets were filled with dates, olives, fruit, and grain. In the south, there were "salt cities." In these places, people built houses out of thick slabs of salt. The roofs were made of camel skin.

Throughout the centuries, various invaders attacked Ghana. Years of plunder and decay would pass. The Arab Muslims tried to force the Ghanians to convert to their religion many times over the years. In 1203, Ghana was attacked by the Sosso tribe who enslaved the Ghanians. Ghana became a weak and powerless country and its capital city was destroyed in 1235.

Mali

Sundiata (Sun-di-ah'-ta) was the leader of the Sosso's who conquered Ghana. In 1240, Sundiata started a professional army that overtook many lands. His kingdom was called Mali. The empire of Mali contained the former Ghana. The kingdom of Mali was larger than all of Europe. Like Ghana, Mali's power came from gold, iron, and salt.

In 1307, Sundiata's grandson became the Sultan of Mali. His name was Mansa Musa (Man-sah' Moo'-sah). During Mansa Musa's reign, Mali became famous throughout the Middle East and Europe. Mansa Musa believed in the Islam religion. In 1324, he decided to make a journey to the spiritual center of his religion in Mecca, Saudia Arabia.

Mansa Musa went on his pilgrimage to Mecca with a caravan of 60,000 men. Musicians played for him while 500 slaves marched in front, each one carrying a four-pound staff made of pure gold. Trains of camels carried gold and gifts. Everywhere he went, Mansa Musa handed out gold to people in the street. In fact, he gave away so much gold that its value dropped. But his generosity and the spectacle of his caravan made Mansa Musa the subject of wonder and gossip for years to come. From Europe to Egypt, Mali was known as a rich and splendid kingdom.

In Mali, Mansa Musa sat on a throne of ebony. On each side, elephant tusks formed an arch over his throne. Above the tusks, a huge, brightly colored umbrella kept the sun off of the sultan's head. By his side stood the fearsome executioner. Clustered around Mansa Musa's throne were trumpeters and drummers. Off to the side stood horses adorned with gold and jewels and soldiers and slaves at attention. From this seat of power, Mansa Musa ruled Mali for many years.

A modern-day sultan on his horse.

Mansa Musa built an incredibile kingdom. Mali was known the world over for its wealthy, well-organized cities. Mali was reknown throughout the western world for its culture and schools. Mansa Musa also put Mali on the map. Around 1350, European mapmakers started showing Mali on their maps and even told travelers how to get there.

After Mansa Musa'a death, the kingdom of Mali grew weaker. Still, 12,000 camels a year traveled over just one of the caravan routes. Other caravans came from every direction. Mali was a peaceful kingdom and several travelers wrote that its people believed in justice. They also said the kingdom was safe. Many travelers said that they felt safer in Mali than in any other city in Europe and the Middle East.

The Fabled City of Timbuktu

In the heart of the kingdom of Mali, on the banks of the Niger River lay the splendid city of Timbuktu (Tim-buk'-too). During Mansa Musa's reign, he had ordered Islamic houses of worship, called mosques (mosks), to be built in Timbuktu. The mosques were incredible buildings with solid gold domes, velvet rugs, fountains, and artwork carved into stone. They were designed by a spanish poet and were said to be as beautiful as any mosques in the world.

Timbuktu was also known as a center for learning. While the Hundred Years War was tearing apart Europe, Timbuktu was in its golden age of knowledge and wisdom. One traveler wrote, "The king pays great respect for men of learning. More profit is made from the book trade than any other line of business."

Timbuktu's glory only lasted several hundred years. What knowledge her scholars possessed is yet to be discovered, for the centuries have faded their books to dust. But during her glory, Timbuktu was a jeweled city in the golden crown of Mali.

The fabled city of Timbukto.

CHAPTER 3
THE FOREST KINGDOMS OF AFRICA

Artwork of the Jungle

South of the merchant kingdoms, the dry grasslands turned into lush, green, tropical forests. Along the equator the rains produced a hodgepodge of beautiful trees and plants. And just like the rain, the people who lived in those forests also produced a dizzying array of beauty. The forest people produced bronze masks, wood carvings, gold jewelry, and more.

The history we know about the merchant kingdoms like Mali comes mostly from Arab traders. But the thick jungle prevented outsiders from exploring the forest kingdoms. Most of what is known about them comes from stories that were passed down from one generation to the next. Archaeologists are also piecing together information to help us find out about the forest kingdoms.

Bronze figure.

The Nok Culture

The oldest culture discovered so far in West Africa is the Nok Culture. Archaeologists have unearthed lifelike statues made from baked clay. The figures are extremely well made. The heads of the statues are three times larger than the bodies. This shows that the Nok people thought the head with its eyes and ears was the most important part of the body. The Nok people seem to be the orginators of African art styles that are used to the present day in Nigeria. The Nok Culture existed about 3,000 years ago. Only their clay work is left to tell us anything about them.

Yoruba

The Yoruba (Yor-oo'-bah) states, near present-day Nigeria, were the largest and most important forest kingdoms in West Africa. The Yoruba are the descendents of the Nok people. Yoruba artwork is known the world over for its beautiful bronze and brass masks and statues. In 1897, British archaeologists discovered bronze statues that are ranked among the greatest art in the world. Some of the finest were thought to be made in the 1400's and to portray the heads of kings.

People in Yoruba lived in walled cities and grew their food in fields that lay outside of the walls. They engaged in trade with kingdoms in the north. Cloth and koala nuts were their main products. After the 1500's the Yoruba people began trading with the Europeans on Africa's west coast. The Europeans came to buy ivory, pepper, and slaves.

The main city in Yoruba was called Benin. The Europeans were impressed with Benin's wide streets and neat rows of houses. A Dutch visitor in 1602 was impressed with the king's palace in Benin. The visitor said the palace had huge rooms with galleries and courtyards. Giant brass statues decorated every room. The Dutch visitor saw the king's horses in their stables and the king's slaves carrying water, yams, and palm wine for their master.

As the years passed, many people were taken from Benin by the Europeans. They were sent to America and forced to become slaves. By the 1700's, Benin was deserted and its buildings crumbled into ruin. The countryside was empty and its cultivated land overgrown and unused.

CHAPTER 4
THE ZANJ KINGDOM OF EAST AFRICA

The Lands of the Zanj

Portuguese explorers sailed down the coast of West Africa in the late 1400's. After they rounded the bottom of the continent at the Cape of Good Hope, they sailed up the eastern coast. Much to their surprise, the Portuguese found civilizations and towns as beautiful as any in Europe. They found cities with tall buildings made of stone and coral, white and sparking in the sun. The Portuguese found ports filled with ships from India and China. Many of the ships were larger and better built than the European ships. The busy trade gave the towns an air of settled wealth and luxury. Much to their surprise, the Portuguese were not treated as important and unexpected guests. The people of the coast were used to visitors arriving from the sea.

Vasco da Gama, the leader of the expedition, wrote in his diary, "When we had been there for three days, two gentlemen of the country came to see us. They were very haughty and valued nothing we gave them." But the Portuguese "cried with joy" at what they saw and heard in the country. They saw it as a place to make their fortunes.

The area described by the Portuguese was a country called the Land of Zanj. Zanj stretched from present-day Mozambique (Mo-zam-beek') to Kenya and included the island of Madagascar (Mad-ah-gas'-ker).

People in Zanj had been trading with China, Arabia, and India for almost two thousand years. The Zanj people killed elephants for their ivory tusks. They traded the ivory for wheat, rice, sesame oil, cotton cloth, and honey. The Europeans also traded with Zanj. Gold Roman coins from the third century have been found in the sands of Zanj. The Zanj also exported gold, tortoise shells, and slaves. Iron mined in Zanj was valued in India. Zanjian ivory was used in China for splendid chairs in which kings would be carried.

As the centuries passed, the people of Zanj imported large amounts of cloth and beads from India. From further east came ships laden with silk, pottery, and porcelain from China. The pottery from China was (and is) very valuable. A shipload of it was worth a lot of money. Between 1200 and 1500, the wealth of the trade between China and Zanj was unequaled anywhere in the world.

The Fall of Zanj

The Portuguese arrival in Zanj was disastrous to the wealthy, easygoing civilizations there. The Portuguese were heavily armed with guns and cannons. They wanted control over the riches of Zanj and they took it. They raided the coastal towns with a cruelty and savageness that the peaceful Zanj people could not resist. The beautiful towns, with centuries of history and culture behind them, were destroyed and their citizens massacred. The gorgeous homes of Zanj were looted and burned by the Portuguese invaders. Today, fragments of pottery and overgrown ruins in the jungle are the only remains left of Zanj. Once, Zanj was the richest kingdom in the world. Today that kingdom has been reduced to dust.

CHAPTER 5
ART, MUSIC, AND GODS

The Artists

African artists expressed devotion to their gods in sculpture, music, and dancing. From the royal masks of the Benin people to the monster masks of other tribes, Africans used their art to express religious traditions. Africans used bronze, wood, clay, cloth, iron, and gold in their artwork. Besides sculpture, pots, and masks, the Africans made jewelry and clothes with great respect for tradition and quality.

African sculpture was seldom enjoyed as art. Each piece was designed to attract different religious spirits. Carved dolls were used to house spirits of unborn babies. Carved drummers were pounded into the ground during dances to awaken the spirits in the earth. Geometric patterns were woven into cloth and painted onto faces. Each pattern had its own religious meaning. Masks that were carved to look like animals or mythical beasts were worn during weddings, funerals, and other ceremonies. Sometimes dancers would go into a trance and take on the spirit of the mask. Masked dancers, feeling themselves possessed by strange spirits, would dance for hours.

Many artists also made cups, stools, spoons, and knives for every day use.

A monster mask to keep the evil spirits away.

A wood cut figure representing a woman with her newborn baby.

The Power of the Gods

There are almost as many African gods as there are African tribes. Nearly all Africans believed in a single "High God" from whom all things flowed. Beneath the High God, lesser gods ruled human affairs. Africans had gods of storms, mountains, rivers, snakes, seas, trees, lions, and just about everything that affected their lives.

Within every tribe, several people were thought to communicate with the gods. Often, these people were skilled in the art of physical and mental healing. Some of their cures for sickness came from plants and herbs.

Africans also worshipped their ancestors. Many dances, songs, and works of art were made to contact relatives long dead. Many Africans believed in scorcery and witchcraft. There was good magic and bad magic. Africans often used witch doctors to help them break evil spells or avoid bad luck.

Although Europeans tried to change the Africans' beliefs, the spiritual African tradition still exists in many parts of the world today.

The Dance and Drums of Africa

To Africans, dancing was the most important art. Dance combined religion and everyday matters. Thus, there were dances to mark the beginning of a hunt and dances for the end. Harvests, marriages, holidays, gods, goddesses, and religious ceremonies all had their own dances. At the heart of all African dances was the drum.

Africans pounded on rocks before they learned how to stretch hides over hollow logs to make drums. A good African drummer could make his drum "speak" in words and sentences that were understood by other tribesman. Drums were used to send messages from one village to the next. A drum message could be sent a hundred miles in two hours by a series of drummers. Many drums were considered sacred and only used in certain religious ceremonies.

A Final Word

The height of African culture was between the tenth and sixteenth centuries. When the Europeans came to Africa, they destroyed almost everything they found. Once the slave trade started, Africa lost over one half of its population to slavery. Over 50 million human beings were kidnapped in their homeland and sent to work in the fields in America. Two-thirds of them died along the way.

The people who dealt in this human misery did not want the world to know the truth about Africa. In the 1500's, most Europeans thought Africa was an untamed jungle filled with savages. They did not know of the scholars, artwork, and civilized society that populated many parts of Africa. Many of these myths continue today. One book cannot describe all the different and wonderful faces of Africa. Local libraries have many more books on African customs, art, and people. By understanding the people, we can make the history of Africa come alive.

**African Art Work
Before the 1600's**

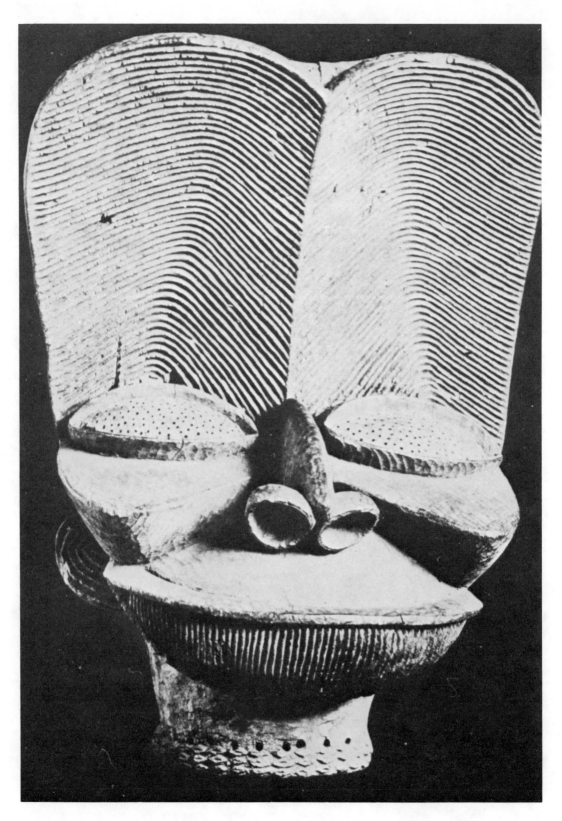

42

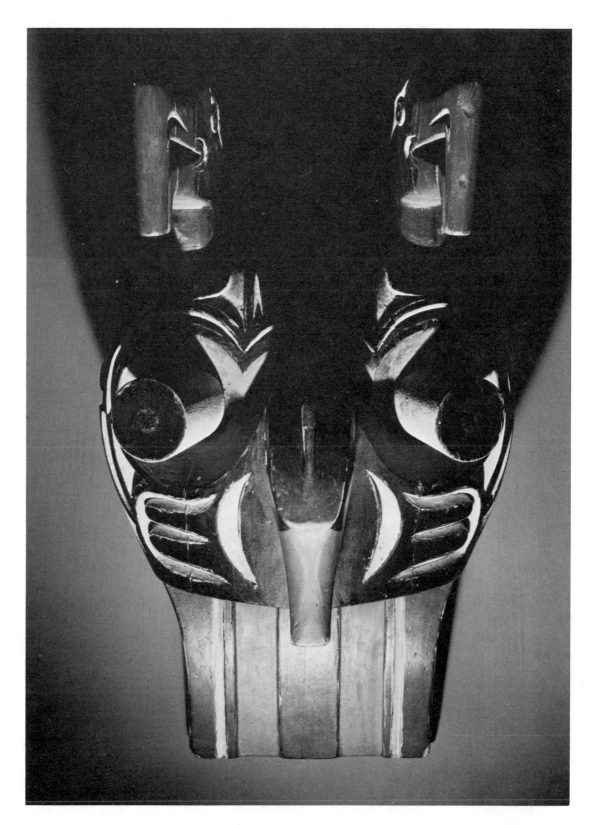

44

INDEX